When I'm At Wo

Refuse Collector

Written by ...e Barraclough

Photography ... Chris Fairclough

First published in 2006 by Franklin Watts
338 Euston Road, London NW1 3BH

Franklin Watts Australia
Hachette Children's Books
Level 17/207 Kent Street
Sydney NSW 2000

Editor: Adrian Cole
Designer: Jemima Lumley
Art direction: Jonathan Hair
Photography: Chris Fairclough

The publisher wishes to thank Giten, Neil, Ken, Chris and Paul at Verdant, John at Colsterworth landfill site, and the pupils and staff of Sea Mills Infant School, Bristol for taking part.

A CIP catalogue record for this book is available from the British Library

ISBN 0 7496 6390 1

Dewey decimal classification number: 628.4

Printed in China

Contents

I am a refuse collector

My name is Giten. I am a refuse collector. My job is to take away rubbish in a big refuse truck.

I work as part of a team. Neil drives the truck. Ken and I collect and empty the bins into the truck.

Starting work

I wait by the depot gates for Neil to arrive. Neil collects the details of today's round.

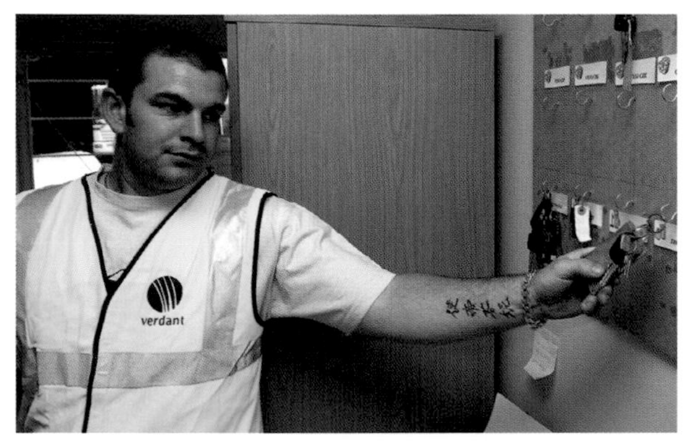

Neil collects the truck keys from the office. We climb into the cab of the truck. Now we are ready to go.

Setting off on the round

First, Neil fills up the truck with fuel. Then we drive to the first stop on our round.

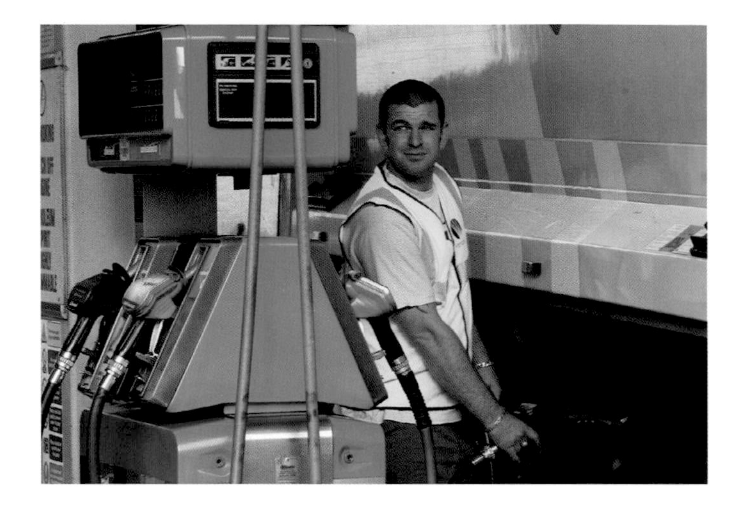

People leave their bins out on the pavement for us to empty. We work our way down the streets. We collect and empty all the bins. Then we put them back where we found them.

Emptying bins

I wheel each bin to the back of the truck. Then I push it on to the bin lifter. The bin lifter picks up the bin and tips the rubbish into the truck.

To make more room for rubbish in the back of the truck, I press a button to crush the rubbish together.

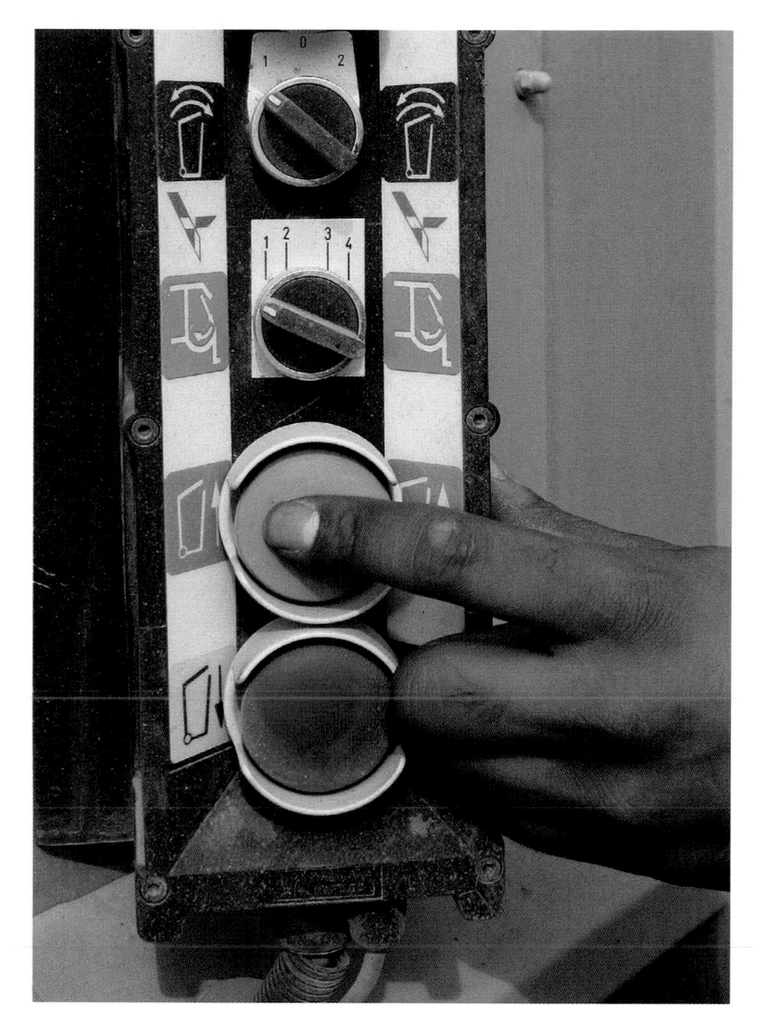

Then I wheel the bin back to the right house, before I collect another one.

Collecting and returning bins

We collect, empty and return the bins as fast as we can. We have a lot more rubbish to take away.

Some ill or elderly people cannot put their bins out on the pavement. So I go into their gardens to collect them. Then I wheel them out to the truck.

Working together

There is a camera on the truck so Neil can see us working behind it. He watches us on a screen in the cab, so he can make sure we are out of the way before he moves the truck.

Sometimes I help Neil to reverse the truck.
I make sure nothing gets in the way.

Filling the truck

We work hard, going from road to road. We collect hundreds of bins and bags full of rubbish.

Neil has a machine in the cab that shows him when the truck is full up. When it is full, we drive to the landfill site.

Going to the landfill site

The landfill site is a huge hole in the ground. When we arrive, we drive on to some huge scales so the truck can be weighed.

We drive down into the landfill site to unload the rubbish. Lots of refuse trucks come and go all day.

To empty the truck Neil puts on a safety hat and gets out of the cab. He presses a button to open the truck. The back of the truck swings open and up.

Emptying the truck

All the rubbish we collected is pushed out into a heap. When the truck is empty, we drive away. Then we can close the back of the truck.

A big bulldozer, called a compactor, pushes and spreads out the rubbish with its huge bulldozer scoop.

The compactor squashes the rubbish with its heavy, spiked wheels.

Then a digger covers the rubbish with soil to stop it blowing away.

Finishing work

When we have finished our round, we drive back to the depot. I wash all the dust and dirt off the truck.

Neil parks the truck, ready to start work tomorrow morning. Then it is time to go home.

Refuse collector equipment

Wheely bins have wheels so they are easy to move around. They have a rim that slots on to the bin lifter.

Collecting rubbish is dirty work, so there is a **handwashing unit** fitted on the side of the truck.

This **jacket** and these **trousers** have special strips to reflect the light. As refuse collectors often work on busy roads, it is important that they can be seen clearly by other road users.

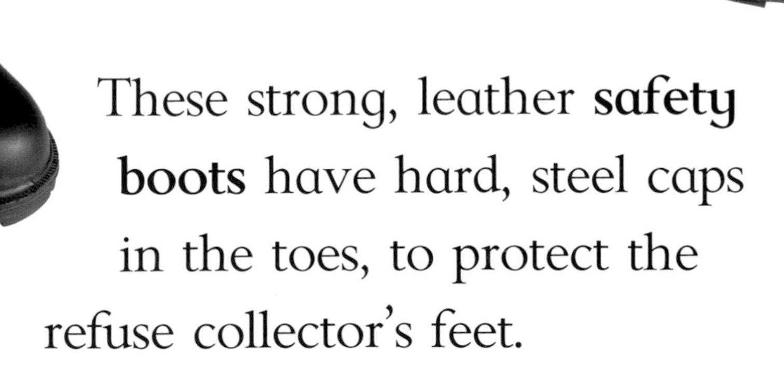

These strong, leather **safety boots** have hard, steel caps in the toes, to protect the refuse collector's feet.

Cut down your rubbish

We send too much rubbish to landfill sites. So we need to cut down the amount of rubbish we put out for collection.

Find out what your local recycling team will collect. It is just as easy as putting out your rubbish bin.

You can cut down and reduce your rubbish by using fruit and vegetable waste to make compost. To find out more go to: **http://www.wasteonline.org.uk** and look at the information sheets.

Glossary and index

Bulldozer scoop - the front part of a bulldozer that pushes things around. **Page 23**

Cab - the front part of a truck where the driver and passengers sit. **Pages 9, 16, 19**

Compost - rotten vegetable and plant waste used to help plants grow. **Page 29**

Depot - a place where things are stored. **Pages 8, 24**

Landfill site - a huge hole in the ground where refuse trucks take rubbish to be buried. **Pages 19, 20, 21, 28**

Reverse - when something, such as a truck, moves backwards. The opposite of forwards. **Page 17**

Round - the route followed by refuse collectors to collect and empty bins. **Pages 8, 10, 24**

Scales - a machine used to measure weight: how heavy or light something is. **Page 20**